Distributed in the United States by
Smart Apple Media,
1980 Lookout Drive,
North Mankato,
Minnesota 56003

Text copyright © Linda Bygrave
Illustrations copyright © Louise Voce

Consultant: Michael Chinery

ISBN 1-93198-351-8
Library of Congress Control Number 2003102392

Printed in China

I am a Tiger

Written By
Linda Bygrave

Illustrated by
Andy Cooke

Chrysalis Education

I am a tiger.

Tigers are the biggest cats
in the world.

I live in the hot jungles of India.

Some tigers live in snowy Siberia.

I have orange fur with black stripes.

The stripes on my face make a pattern.

Each tiger has a different pattern.

I have really big teeth and claws
because I am a hunter.
The animals I hunt are called my prey.

I can pull my claws inside my paws,
just like a house cat.

I can pad very quietly
through the hot, steamy jungle.

I like to live on my own.

I have my own area to hunt in.

It's called my territory.

In my territory I scratch trees
and leave my smell.
The smell tells other tigers that I live here.

I love to play and swim in water.

When I feel hot I lie in cool, shallow pools.

I am a female tiger.

Over there are two male tigers.

They are fighting over me!
The winner will be the father of my cubs.

About three months later my cubs are born.

I might have two or three or even four cubs.

Aren't they tiny?

I look after them in a safe place.

Their daddy doesn't help me.

He goes back to his own territory.

My babies drink my milk at first.
Then I start bringing them meat
from my hunting trips.

If I'm worried about them, I carry them
in my mouth to a safer place.

My cubs practice hunting while they play.
Soon, they will come hunting with me.

Hunting is very dangerous for my cubs.

They must stay very close to me.

They meow loudly if they get lost!

When my cubs are about one year old,
I teach them how to hunt for themselves.

In another year my cubs will leave home.
They'll have their own families one day.

There aren't many of us left these days.
We were hunted by people, and now
our forests are being cut down.

Luckily, special places called nature
reserves are being made so we can live
in safety. I fancy a nap now . . . Good-bye!